EMMANUEL JOSEPH

The Wellness Analogy, How Politics, Society, and Psychology Influence Health and Commerce

Copyright © 2025 by Emmanuel Joseph

All rights reserved. No part of this publication may be reproduced, stored or transmitted in any form or by any means, electronic, mechanical, photocopying, recording, scanning, or otherwise without written permission from the publisher. It is illegal to copy this book, post it to a website, or distribute it by any other means without permission.

First edition

This book was professionally typeset on Reedsy.
Find out more at reedsy.com

Contents

1. Chapter 1: The Interwoven Fabric of Politics and Health — 1
2. Chapter 2: Society's Role in Shaping Health — 3
3. Chapter 3: The Psychological Dimension of Health — 5
4. Chapter 4: The Intersection of Commerce and Health — 7
5. Chapter 5: Health Inequities and Social Justice — 9
6. Chapter 6: The Role of Media in Health Perception — 11
7. Chapter 7: Economic Policies and Public Health — 13
8. Chapter 8: Education and Health Literacy — 15
9. Chapter 9: The Globalization of Health — 17
10. Chapter 10: Health and Environmental Sustainability — 19
11. Chapter 11: Technology and Health — 21
12. Chapter 12: The Impact of Public Health Campaigns — 23
13. Chapter 13: Mental Health and Society — 25
14. Chapter 14: The Role of Innovation in Health — 27
15. Chapter 15: Health Policy and Advocacy — 30
16. Chapter 16: The Future of Health and Commerce — 32
17. Chapter 17: The Path Forward: Integrating Health and... — 34

1

Chapter 1: The Interwoven Fabric of Politics and Health

In the grand tapestry of human society, the influence of politics on health is akin to the intricate weaving of a fabric. Political decisions, policies, and governance structures can either strengthen the threads of health and well-being or fray them, leading to disparities and inequities. Governments play a crucial role in shaping healthcare systems, determining the allocation of resources, and establishing public health priorities. From universal healthcare initiatives to vaccination campaigns, political actions have a direct impact on the accessibility and quality of healthcare services available to the population.

Political ideologies and agendas also influence public health outcomes. Policies that prioritize economic growth over social welfare may lead to underfunded healthcare systems and reduced access to essential services. Conversely, governments that prioritize social equity and invest in public health infrastructure tend to have healthier populations. The intersection of politics and health is evident in the way policies address social determinants of health, such as education, housing, and income inequality. Political will and leadership are critical in addressing these determinants and creating an environment conducive to health and well-being.

Furthermore, political stability and governance directly affect the ability of a nation to respond to health crises. The COVID-19 pandemic highlighted the importance of effective political leadership and international cooperation in managing public health emergencies. Countries with robust political systems and transparent governance were better equipped to implement measures to control the spread of the virus and support their healthcare systems. On the other hand, political instability and corruption can undermine public health efforts, leading to inadequate responses and increased vulnerability to health threats.

In essence, politics and health are inextricably linked, with political decisions shaping the health landscape of nations. Understanding this relationship is crucial for advocating for policies that promote health equity and well-being. As we navigate the complexities of modern society, it is essential to recognize the role of politics in influencing health outcomes and work towards creating a political environment that prioritizes the health and welfare of all individuals.

2

Chapter 2: Society's Role in Shaping Health

Society is the backdrop against which the drama of human health unfolds. The cultural norms, social structures, and community relationships within any given society play a pivotal role in determining health outcomes. At the heart of societal influence is the concept of social determinants of health, which encompasses factors such as socioeconomic status, education, neighborhood and physical environment, employment, and social support networks.

Socioeconomic status is a powerful determinant of health. Individuals and communities with higher socioeconomic status often have better access to healthcare, nutritious food, safe housing, and educational opportunities. These advantages contribute to healthier lifestyles and better health outcomes. Conversely, those in lower socioeconomic brackets may face barriers to accessing healthcare and other resources, leading to disparities in health. Addressing these inequalities requires a multi-faceted approach that includes policy interventions, community engagement, and social support programs.

Education is another critical factor in societal health. Education equips individuals with the knowledge and skills necessary to make informed health choices. It also opens doors to better employment opportunities, which in turn can provide the financial stability needed to maintain good health.

Communities with higher levels of education tend to have lower rates of chronic diseases and higher life expectancies. Efforts to improve educational opportunities and reduce educational disparities are essential for promoting public health.

The physical environment, including housing, transportation, and neighborhood infrastructure, significantly impacts health. Safe and clean living conditions, access to recreational spaces, and availability of healthy food options contribute to the overall well-being of individuals. On the other hand, living in areas with poor air quality, limited access to healthcare, and high crime rates can adversely affect health. Urban planning and community development initiatives that prioritize health and safety can create environments that support healthier lifestyles.

Social support networks and community relationships are also vital for health. Strong social ties can provide emotional support, reduce stress, and promote healthy behaviors. Communities that foster a sense of belonging and social cohesion tend to have better health outcomes. Conversely, social isolation and lack of community support can lead to negative health consequences. Building inclusive and supportive communities through social programs, community organizations, and public policies is essential for enhancing public health.

In conclusion, society's role in shaping health is profound and multifaceted. By addressing the social determinants of health and fostering supportive community environments, we can create a society that promotes health and well-being for all its members.

3

Chapter 3: The Psychological Dimension of Health

Psychology plays a critical role in shaping health outcomes, influencing everything from individual behaviors to the collective well-being of communities. Understanding the psychological underpinnings of health requires an examination of how thoughts, emotions, and behaviors interact with physical health. Mental health is not an isolated aspect of well-being but rather an integral component of overall health.

Stress is a fundamental psychological factor that affects health. Chronic stress can lead to a variety of physical health problems, including heart disease, hypertension, and weakened immune function. The sources of stress are diverse, ranging from work-related pressures to personal relationships and financial concerns. Effective stress management techniques, such as mindfulness, exercise, and relaxation practices, are essential for maintaining mental and physical health. Public health initiatives that promote mental health awareness and provide resources for stress management can have a significant impact on overall health outcomes.

Behavioral psychology also plays a crucial role in health. Health behaviors, such as diet, exercise, and substance use, are influenced by psychological factors, including motivation, self-efficacy, and habits. Positive health behaviors can be encouraged through interventions that address these psychological aspects. For example, programs that promote healthy eating and physical activity often include components that build motivation and self-efficacy, helping individuals make and sustain healthy lifestyle changes. Understanding the psychological drivers of health behaviors is key to developing effective public health interventions.

The impact of psychological well-being on physical health is also evident in the mind-body connection. Psychological conditions, such as depression and anxiety, can exacerbate physical health problems and hinder recovery. Conversely, positive psychological states, such as happiness and optimism, are associated with better health outcomes and longer life expectancy. Integrating mental health care into primary care and other healthcare settings can improve the overall health of individuals by addressing both physical and psychological needs.

Community psychology emphasizes the importance of social support and community relationships in promoting health. Social connections and a sense of belonging can buffer against stress and contribute to better mental health. Community-based interventions that foster social support networks and promote community engagement can enhance psychological well-being and overall health. Efforts to build resilient communities that support mental health can lead to healthier, more connected populations.

In summary, psychology is a critical dimension of health, influencing individual behaviors, stress management, and the mind-body connection. By addressing psychological factors and promoting mental health, we can improve overall health outcomes and create healthier communities.

4

Chapter 4: The Intersection of Commerce and Health

Commerce and health are interconnected in ways that impact individuals and societies on multiple levels. The healthcare industry itself is a significant economic sector, with implications for job creation, innovation, and economic growth. Additionally, the relationship between commerce and health extends to how businesses influence health behaviors and outcomes through the products and services they offer.

The healthcare industry is a major driver of economic activity. Hospitals, clinics, pharmaceutical companies, and medical device manufacturers create millions of jobs and contribute to the economic well-being of communities. Investment in healthcare infrastructure and research fosters innovation, leading to advancements in medical technology and treatments. However, the commercial aspect of healthcare can also introduce challenges, such as the rising cost of medical care and the accessibility of services. Balancing the economic interests of healthcare providers with the need to ensure affordable and equitable access to care is a critical issue that policymakers and industry leaders must address.

The influence of commerce on health extends beyond the healthcare industry to the broader marketplace. Businesses play a significant role in shaping health behaviors through the products and services they offer.

The food and beverage industry, for example, has a profound impact on dietary habits and nutrition. Marketing strategies and product availability can influence consumer choices, leading to either positive or negative health outcomes. Companies that prioritize health and wellness by offering nutritious products and promoting healthy lifestyles can contribute to improved public health. On the other hand, the promotion of unhealthy products, such as sugary beverages and processed foods, can exacerbate health issues like obesity and diabetes.

Corporate social responsibility (CSR) is an important consideration in the intersection of commerce and health. Companies that embrace CSR initiatives can positively impact public health by addressing social determinants of health and supporting community well-being. Examples of CSR initiatives include funding healthcare programs, creating healthy workplace environments, and engaging in sustainable business practices. By integrating health considerations into their business models, companies can contribute to the overall health and well-being of society while also enhancing their reputation and brand value.

The relationship between commerce and health also highlights the importance of consumer advocacy and regulatory oversight. Consumers play a crucial role in demanding healthier products and holding companies accountable for their impact on public health. Regulatory agencies, such as the Food and Drug Administration (FDA) and the World Health Organization (WHO), are essential in setting standards and guidelines to ensure the safety and efficacy of products in the marketplace. Collaborative efforts between businesses, consumers, and regulators are necessary to create a commercial environment that supports health and wellness.

In summary, commerce and health are intricately linked, with the healthcare industry driving economic activity and businesses influencing health behaviors and outcomes. By fostering a commercial environment that prioritizes health and wellness, we can create a healthier society and promote sustainable economic growth.

5

Chapter 5: Health Inequities and Social Justice

Health inequities are differences in health outcomes that are systematic, avoidable, and unjust. These inequities often stem from social, economic, and environmental disparities, leading to unfair disadvantages for certain groups. Addressing health inequities requires a focus on social justice, which involves ensuring fair treatment, opportunities, and outcomes for all individuals, regardless of their background or circumstances.

Social justice in health involves recognizing and addressing the root causes of health disparities. These causes include factors such as poverty, discrimination, and lack of access to healthcare. For example, marginalized communities may face barriers to accessing quality healthcare due to financial constraints, geographic isolation, or systemic racism. Addressing these barriers requires targeted interventions that promote equity and inclusivity. Policies and programs that provide affordable healthcare, improve education, and create economic opportunities can help reduce health disparities and promote social justice.

Another critical aspect of social justice in health is addressing the social determinants of health. These determinants include factors such as housing, education, employment, and social support, which influence health outcomes.

Ensuring that all individuals have access to safe and affordable housing, quality education, and stable employment can contribute to better health outcomes and reduce health inequities. Additionally, promoting social support networks and fostering inclusive communities can enhance social cohesion and improve overall well-being.

Health equity also involves addressing the intersectionality of various social identities and their impact on health. Individuals may experience compounded disadvantages based on their race, gender, sexual orientation, disability, or other intersecting identities. For example, women of color may face unique challenges that affect their health, such as higher rates of maternal mortality and limited access to reproductive healthcare. Addressing health inequities requires a comprehensive approach that considers the diverse experiences and needs of different populations.

Advocacy and community engagement are essential components of promoting social justice in health. Empowering individuals and communities to advocate for their health rights and participate in decision-making processes can lead to more equitable and effective health policies. Grassroots movements, community organizations, and advocacy groups play a crucial role in raising awareness, mobilizing resources, and driving change. Collaborative efforts that involve multiple stakeholders, including policymakers, healthcare providers, and community members, are necessary to address health inequities and promote social justice.

In summary, addressing health inequities requires a focus on social justice, which involves ensuring fair treatment, opportunities, and outcomes for all individuals. By recognizing and addressing the root causes of health disparities, promoting social determinants of health, and fostering inclusive communities, we can create a more equitable and just society.

6

Chapter 6: The Role of Media in Health Perception

The media wields substantial influence over public perception, shaping beliefs, attitudes, and behaviors related to health. From news outlets to social media platforms, the ways in which health information is disseminated and consumed can have far-reaching implications for individual and public health outcomes.

One of the primary roles of the media is to inform the public about health issues. Accurate and timely reporting on health topics can raise awareness, educate, and empower individuals to make informed decisions about their health. For example, media coverage of public health campaigns, such as vaccination drives and anti-smoking initiatives, can increase participation and contribute to positive health outcomes. However, the media's role in health communication is a double-edged sword. Misinformation and sensationalism can lead to confusion, fear, and harmful behaviors. Ensuring the accuracy and credibility of health information is crucial for maintaining public trust and promoting health literacy.

The media also plays a role in shaping societal norms and expectations related to health and wellness. Television shows, movies, advertisements, and social media influencers contribute to the portrayal of ideal body images, health behaviors, and lifestyle choices. These portrayals can have both positive and negative effects on health. On one hand, media representations of healthy lifestyles and fitness can motivate individuals to adopt healthier behaviors. On the other hand, unrealistic beauty standards and the glorification of certain behaviors, such as excessive dieting or risky health practices, can lead to negative health outcomes, including eating disorders and mental health issues.

Social media, in particular, has transformed the landscape of health communication. Platforms like Instagram, Facebook, and Twitter provide opportunities for individuals to share their health journeys, connect with others, and access a wealth of health-related content. However, the rapid dissemination of information on social media also poses challenges. Misinformation and unverified health advice can spread quickly, potentially leading to harmful consequences. The influence of social media influencers, who may not have formal health training, can further complicate the landscape of health information. Promoting digital literacy and encouraging critical evaluation of online health content are essential for navigating the complexities of social media.

The media's role in health perception extends to the framing of health issues and the portrayal of health disparities. The way in which health stories are reported can influence public understanding and policy responses. Media coverage that highlights health disparities and social determinants of health can raise awareness and advocate for policy changes. Conversely, media narratives that stigmatize certain health conditions or populations can perpetuate stereotypes and discrimination. Ethical and responsible journalism is essential for promoting an inclusive and accurate representation of health issues.

In summary, the media plays a pivotal role in shaping health perception through the dissemination of information, portrayal of health norms, and framing of health issues. By promoting accurate, credible, and inclusive health communication, the media can contribute to better health outcomes and a more informed public.

7

Chapter 7: Economic Policies and Public Health

Economic policies have a profound impact on public health, shaping the financial landscape in which healthcare systems operate and influencing the social determinants of health. Government decisions related to taxation, public spending, and economic regulation can either enhance or hinder the well-being of a population. Understanding the relationship between economic policies and health outcomes is crucial for promoting equitable and sustainable health systems.

Taxation policies play a significant role in funding public health initiatives and healthcare services. Progressive taxation systems, where higher-income individuals and corporations pay a greater share of taxes, can generate revenue to support universal healthcare programs, public health campaigns, and social services. By redistributing wealth and reducing income inequality, progressive taxation can contribute to improved health outcomes for disadvantaged populations. Conversely, regressive taxation policies, which disproportionately burden lower-income individuals, can exacerbate health disparities and limit access to essential services.

Public spending on healthcare is a critical determinant of health outcomes. Governments that allocate sufficient resources to healthcare infrastructure, medical research, and public health programs can create robust and resilient health systems. Investment in primary care, preventive services, and mental health support can lead to better population health and reduced healthcare costs in the long run. However, austerity measures and cuts to healthcare spending can undermine the quality and accessibility of services, leading to negative health consequences. Ensuring adequate and sustainable funding for healthcare is essential for maintaining a healthy and productive society.

Economic regulation also influences public health by shaping the behavior of businesses and industries. Regulatory policies that promote health and safety standards, environmental protection, and consumer rights can protect individuals from health hazards and promote healthy living environments. For example, regulations on tobacco and alcohol sales, food safety standards, and environmental pollution controls can prevent harmful exposures and reduce the burden of disease. Effective enforcement of regulations is necessary to ensure compliance and protect public health.

The interplay between economic policies and health extends to the labor market and employment conditions. Policies that promote fair wages, job security, and safe working conditions can contribute to better health outcomes for workers. Employment provides financial stability, social identity, and access to health benefits, all of which are essential for maintaining good health. Conversely, unemployment, job insecurity, and poor working conditions can lead to stress, mental health issues, and physical health problems. Addressing labor market inequalities and promoting decent work are key components of public health strategies.

In summary, economic policies have a profound impact on public health by influencing taxation, public spending, economic regulation, and labor market conditions. By adopting policies that promote equity, sustainability, and social well-being, governments can create an environment that supports the health and prosperity of all individuals.

8

Chapter 8: Education and Health Literacy

Education is a cornerstone of public health, playing a vital role in promoting health literacy and empowering individuals to make informed health decisions. Health literacy involves the ability to understand and use health information to make choices that promote well-being. It is an essential component of health equity, as higher levels of health literacy are associated with better health outcomes and reduced health disparities.

Education systems can foster health literacy by integrating health education into school curricula. Comprehensive health education programs that cover topics such as nutrition, physical activity, mental health, and substance abuse can equip students with the knowledge and skills needed to lead healthy lives. These programs can also promote critical thinking and decision-making abilities, enabling students to evaluate health information and make informed choices. By prioritizing health education, schools can contribute to the overall well-being of their students and create a foundation for lifelong health literacy.

Health literacy is not limited to formal education settings; it extends to community and public health initiatives as well. Public health campaigns that provide clear, accessible, and culturally relevant information can enhance health literacy among diverse populations. Effective communication strategies, such as using plain language, visual aids, and community engagement, can help bridge the gap between health information and public understanding. Health literacy initiatives that target vulnerable and underserved communities are particularly important for reducing health disparities and promoting equity.

Technology and digital tools also play a crucial role in health literacy. The internet and mobile devices have made health information more accessible than ever before. Online health resources, mobile health apps, and telehealth services can provide individuals with convenient access to health information and support. However, the vast amount of information available online also poses challenges, such as the spread of misinformation and the difficulty of discerning credible sources. Promoting digital health literacy, which involves the ability to navigate and critically evaluate online health information, is essential for empowering individuals in the digital age.

Healthcare providers have a significant role in promoting health literacy as well. Clear communication between healthcare professionals and patients is crucial for ensuring that patients understand their health conditions, treatment options, and preventive measures. Healthcare providers can use strategies such as teach-back methods, visual aids, and patient-centered communication to enhance understanding and support informed decision-making. By fostering a culture of health literacy within healthcare settings, providers can improve patient outcomes and enhance the overall quality of care.

In summary, education and health literacy are fundamental to public health and health equity. By integrating health education into school curricula, promoting community and public health initiatives, leveraging technology, and fostering clear communication in healthcare settings, we can empower individuals to make informed health decisions and create a healthier society.

9

Chapter 9: The Globalization of Health

Globalization has interconnected the world in unprecedented ways, influencing health and commerce on a global scale. The exchange of goods, services, information, and people across borders has profound implications for public health, shaping both opportunities and challenges. Understanding the impact of globalization on health requires an examination of its multifaceted dimensions, including trade, migration, and the spread of information.

Trade and commerce are central components of globalization, affecting health through the availability and affordability of goods and services. The global supply chain enables the distribution of medical supplies, pharmaceuticals, and healthcare technologies, enhancing the capacity of healthcare systems worldwide. Access to affordable medications and advanced medical technologies can improve health outcomes and reduce mortality rates. However, globalization also raises concerns about the quality and safety of imported goods. Regulatory frameworks and international cooperation are essential to ensure that products entering the global market meet safety standards and do not pose health risks.

Migration is another significant aspect of globalization that impacts health. The movement of people across borders contributes to the exchange of knowledge, skills, and cultures, enriching healthcare practices and expanding access to specialized medical care. Migrant health workers play a crucial role in addressing workforce shortages and improving healthcare delivery in many countries. However, migration also presents challenges, such as the spread of infectious diseases and the strain on healthcare resources in receiving countries. Ensuring the health and well-being of migrant populations requires policies that address their unique needs and promote equitable access to healthcare services.

The spread of information through digital and communication technologies is a hallmark of globalization, transforming the way health information is shared and accessed. The internet and social media platforms facilitate the rapid dissemination of health knowledge, enabling individuals to stay informed about health trends, prevention strategies, and treatment options. Telemedicine and digital health tools have expanded access to healthcare, particularly in remote and underserved areas. However, the global flow of information also necessitates vigilance against misinformation and the need for digital literacy to critically evaluate health content.

Global health initiatives and international cooperation are essential for addressing global health challenges. Organizations such as the World Health Organization (WHO), the United Nations (UN), and various non-governmental organizations (NGOs) play a pivotal role in coordinating efforts to combat infectious diseases, improve maternal and child health, and address health disparities. Collaborative approaches that leverage the expertise and resources of multiple stakeholders can lead to more effective and sustainable health interventions. Additionally, global health diplomacy and international agreements are crucial for addressing transnational health issues and promoting global health equity.

In summary, globalization has a profound impact on health and commerce, creating both opportunities and challenges. By leveraging the benefits of globalization while addressing its risks, we can enhance global health outcomes and promote a more interconnected and equitable world.

10

Chapter 10: Health and Environmental Sustainability

The relationship between health and environmental sustainability is integral to the well-being of individuals and communities. Environmental factors, such as air quality, water resources, and climate change, have direct and indirect effects on health. Promoting environmental sustainability is essential for protecting public health and ensuring a healthy planet for future generations.

Air quality is a critical determinant of health, as exposure to air pollution can lead to respiratory and cardiovascular diseases. Emissions from industrial activities, transportation, and agriculture contribute to the release of pollutants, including particulate matter, nitrogen oxides, and sulfur dioxide. Addressing air pollution requires the implementation of clean air policies, the adoption of green technologies, and the promotion of sustainable transportation options. Reducing air pollution not only benefits public health but also contributes to mitigating climate change.

Water resources are another vital aspect of environmental health. Access to clean and safe drinking water is fundamental for preventing waterborne diseases and ensuring overall health. Contamination of water sources due to industrial waste, agricultural runoff, and inadequate sanitation infrastructure poses significant health risks. Efforts to improve water quality and sanitation, such as the development of water treatment facilities and the promotion of hygiene practices, are essential for protecting public health. Sustainable water management practices that prioritize conservation and reduce pollution can help ensure the availability of clean water for all.

Climate change is a global environmental challenge with far-reaching health implications. Rising temperatures, changing weather patterns, and extreme weather events can exacerbate health problems, such as heat-related illnesses, vector-borne diseases, and food and water insecurity. Vulnerable populations, including children, the elderly, and low-income communities, are disproportionately affected by the health impacts of climate change. Mitigation and adaptation strategies, such as reducing greenhouse gas emissions, enhancing climate resilience, and promoting sustainable agriculture, are crucial for addressing the health effects of climate change.

Environmental sustainability also involves the protection of natural ecosystems and biodiversity, which are essential for maintaining the balance of our planet's health. Ecosystems provide valuable services, such as air and water purification, pollination, and climate regulation, which support human health and well-being. Deforestation, habitat destruction, and pollution threaten these ecosystems and the services they provide. Conservation efforts that protect natural habitats, restore degraded ecosystems, and promote sustainable land use practices are vital for safeguarding environmental health.

In summary, the relationship between health and environmental sustainability is integral to public health and the well-being of our planet. By addressing environmental factors such as air quality, water resources, and climate change, we can protect health and promote a sustainable future for all.

11

Chapter 11: Technology and Health

Technology has revolutionized the field of health, bringing about advancements that have transformed healthcare delivery, disease prevention, and patient care. From telemedicine to wearable health devices, the integration of technology into healthcare has the potential to improve health outcomes and increase access to care. However, the rapid pace of technological innovation also presents challenges that must be addressed to ensure equitable and effective use of technology in health.

Telemedicine is one of the most significant advancements in healthcare technology. It allows healthcare providers to deliver care remotely through video consultations, phone calls, and online platforms. Telemedicine has expanded access to healthcare, particularly for individuals in remote or underserved areas. It offers convenience and flexibility for patients, reducing the need for travel and minimizing wait times. During the COVID-19 pandemic, telemedicine played a crucial role in maintaining continuity of care while minimizing the risk of virus transmission. The adoption of telemedicine continues to grow, with ongoing efforts to integrate it into routine healthcare practices and address regulatory and reimbursement challenges.

Wearable health devices and mobile health applications have also gained popularity, empowering individuals to monitor their health and engage in self-care. Devices such as fitness trackers, smartwatches, and health apps can track vital signs, physical activity, sleep patterns, and other health metrics. These tools provide real-time data and personalized insights, helping users make informed decisions about their health. The use of wearable devices for chronic disease management, such as monitoring blood glucose levels in diabetes patients, has shown promising results in improving health outcomes. However, concerns about data privacy and security must be addressed to ensure the safe and ethical use of health technology.

Artificial intelligence (AI) and machine learning are transforming healthcare by enhancing diagnostic accuracy, predicting disease outbreaks, and optimizing treatment plans. AI-powered tools can analyze vast amounts of medical data, identifying patterns and trends that may not be apparent to human clinicians. For example, AI algorithms can assist radiologists in detecting abnormalities in medical images, leading to earlier and more accurate diagnoses. AI is also being used to develop personalized treatment plans based on genetic and clinical data, offering the potential for precision medicine. While AI holds great promise, it is essential to ensure transparency, accountability, and fairness in its application to avoid biases and ensure equitable access to AI-driven healthcare.

The integration of electronic health records (EHRs) has streamlined healthcare administration and improved patient care coordination. EHRs provide a centralized repository of patient information, allowing healthcare providers to access and share data seamlessly. This enhances communication among care teams, reduces duplication of tests and procedures, and improves the quality of care. However, the implementation of EHR systems requires careful planning and investment in infrastructure, training, and cybersecurity measures to protect patient information.

In summary, technology has the potential to revolutionize healthcare, improving access, efficiency, and outcomes. By addressing the challenges and ethical considerations associated with health technology, we can harness its benefits to create a more effective and equitable healthcare system.

12

Chapter 12: The Impact of Public Health Campaigns

Public health campaigns are essential tools for promoting health and preventing disease on a population level. These campaigns use a variety of strategies to raise awareness, change behaviors, and influence public policies. Effective public health campaigns can lead to significant improvements in health outcomes and contribute to the overall well-being of communities.

One of the primary goals of public health campaigns is to raise awareness about health issues and encourage preventive behaviors. Campaigns that target behaviors such as smoking cessation, vaccination, and healthy eating have had a substantial impact on public health. For example, anti-smoking campaigns that use mass media, community engagement, and policy interventions have contributed to a decline in smoking rates and a reduction in smoking-related diseases. Similarly, vaccination campaigns have played a crucial role in preventing infectious diseases and achieving high immunization coverage.

Behavior change is a central component of many public health campaigns. Social marketing techniques, which apply marketing principles to promote health behaviors, are often used to design and implement these campaigns. Strategies such as persuasive messaging, social norms marketing, and incentives can motivate individuals to adopt healthier behaviors. For example, campaigns that promote physical activity may use motivational messages, community events, and rewards to encourage people to exercise regularly. By understanding the psychological and social factors that influence behavior, public health campaigns can effectively drive behavior change and improve health outcomes.

Public health campaigns also play a critical role in shaping public policies and creating supportive environments for health. Advocacy efforts that highlight the health impacts of social determinants, such as housing, education, and income, can influence policy decisions and promote health equity. For example, campaigns that advocate for policies to reduce air pollution or increase access to healthy food options can create healthier environments and reduce health disparities. Collaboration with policymakers, community leaders, and stakeholders is essential for the success of these advocacy efforts.

Evaluation and measurement are crucial for assessing the effectiveness of public health campaigns. Monitoring and evaluating campaign outcomes, such as changes in knowledge, attitudes, behaviors, and health indicators, provide valuable insights into what works and what does not. This information can guide the development of future campaigns and ensure that resources are used efficiently. Continuous evaluation and adaptation of campaign strategies are essential for achieving sustained health improvements.

In conclusion, public health campaigns are powerful tools for promoting health and preventing disease. By raising awareness, changing behaviors, and influencing public policies, these campaigns can lead to significant improvements in health outcomes and contribute to the overall well-being of communities.

13

Chapter 13: Mental Health and Society

Mental health is a critical component of overall well-being, yet it has often been stigmatized and neglected within society. Understanding the societal factors that influence mental health is essential for creating supportive environments and promoting mental wellness. Mental health issues, such as depression, anxiety, and substance use disorders, affect individuals from all walks of life and can have profound implications for families, communities, and society as a whole.

Stigma surrounding mental health is one of the most significant barriers to seeking help and support. Negative attitudes and misconceptions about mental health conditions can lead to discrimination, social isolation, and reluctance to access treatment. Addressing stigma requires public awareness campaigns, education, and open conversations about mental health. By challenging stereotypes and promoting understanding, we can create a more inclusive society that supports individuals experiencing mental health challenges.

Socioeconomic factors also play a crucial role in mental health. Poverty, unemployment, and financial insecurity can contribute to stress, anxiety, and depression. Individuals facing economic hardships may have limited access to mental health services and support networks, exacerbating their mental health issues. Addressing the social determinants of mental health, such as income inequality and job opportunities, is essential for promoting mental wellness. Policies that provide financial assistance, job training, and affordable housing can help reduce the mental health burden associated with socioeconomic disadvantages.

The role of family and social support is vital for mental health. Strong social connections and supportive relationships can provide emotional support, reduce stress, and promote resilience. Families and communities that foster open communication and empathy can create a safe environment for individuals to share their struggles and seek help. Community-based mental health programs and peer support groups can also play a significant role in providing accessible and culturally relevant support.

Access to mental health services is a critical factor in addressing mental health issues. Barriers to access, such as cost, lack of insurance coverage, and geographic limitations, can prevent individuals from receiving the care they need. Expanding access to mental health services through public funding, insurance coverage, and telehealth options can improve mental health outcomes. Integrating mental health care into primary care settings and offering community-based services can also enhance accessibility and reduce stigma.

In summary, mental health is deeply influenced by societal factors, including stigma, socioeconomic conditions, social support, and access to services. By addressing these factors and promoting a supportive and inclusive society, we can improve mental health outcomes and enhance overall well-being.

14

Chapter 14: The Role of Innovation in Health

Innovation is a driving force behind advancements in health and healthcare, leading to new treatments, technologies, and approaches that improve patient outcomes and quality of life. The pursuit of innovation in health encompasses a wide range of fields, including medical research, biotechnology, digital health, and public health strategies. Embracing innovation is essential for addressing emerging health challenges and ensuring a resilient and adaptive healthcare system.

Medical research and biotechnology are at the forefront of health innovation. Breakthroughs in genetics, molecular biology, and pharmacology have led to the development of new diagnostic tools, therapies, and vaccines. Precision medicine, which tailors treatments based on an individual's genetic makeup and clinical profile, holds promise for improving the efficacy and safety of medical interventions. Advances in biotechnology, such as gene editing and regenerative medicine, offer the potential to treat and even cure previously untreatable conditions. Continued investment in medical research and collaboration between academic institutions, industry, and government agencies are crucial for fostering innovation and translating discoveries into clinical practice.

Digital health technologies, including telemedicine, wearable devices, and health apps, have transformed the way healthcare is delivered and experienced. These technologies enable remote monitoring, personalized health management, and real-time data analysis, enhancing patient engagement and empowerment. Telemedicine has expanded access to care, particularly in rural and underserved areas, while wearable devices provide valuable insights into an individual's health behaviors and physiological parameters. The integration of digital health technologies into healthcare systems can improve care coordination, efficiency, and outcomes. However, addressing challenges related to data privacy, interoperability, and equity is essential for maximizing the benefits of digital health.

Public health innovation involves developing and implementing new strategies to address population health challenges. Innovative public health approaches, such as community-based interventions, social marketing campaigns, and health policy reforms, can improve health behaviors and outcomes. For example, community health worker programs that provide culturally competent care and support can enhance healthcare access and health literacy in marginalized communities. Public health innovation also includes leveraging data analytics and epidemiological tools to track health trends, predict disease outbreaks, and inform policy decisions. Collaborative efforts between public health organizations, policymakers, and community stakeholders are vital for driving innovation and achieving public health goals.

Innovation in health is not limited to technological advancements; it also encompasses new models of care delivery and organizational practices. Patient-centered care, which focuses on meeting the individual needs and preferences of patients, has gained traction as a transformative approach to healthcare. Value-based care models, which prioritize health outcomes and cost-effectiveness, are reshaping healthcare reimbursement and delivery systems. Innovations in care coordination, interdisciplinary collaboration, and healthcare management can enhance the efficiency and effectiveness of healthcare services.

In conclusion, innovation is a key driver of progress in health and healthcare. By fostering a culture of innovation and embracing new technologies, approaches, and models of care, we can address emerging health challenges, improve patient outcomes, and enhance the overall quality of healthcare.

15

Chapter 15: Health Policy and Advocacy

Health policy plays a pivotal role in shaping the healthcare landscape and determining health outcomes. Effective health policies address the needs of the population, promote health equity, and ensure the sustainability of healthcare systems. Advocacy efforts are essential for influencing health policy decisions and driving positive change. By engaging in health policy and advocacy, individuals and organizations can contribute to the creation of a more just and equitable healthcare system.

Health policies encompass a wide range of areas, including healthcare access, quality of care, public health, and health system financing. Policies that promote universal healthcare coverage and reduce financial barriers to care are fundamental for ensuring that all individuals have access to necessary health services. Health insurance reforms, such as the expansion of Medicaid and the establishment of health insurance marketplaces, have been instrumental in increasing healthcare coverage and reducing uninsured rates. Ensuring that healthcare policies prioritize the needs of marginalized and vulnerable populations is essential for achieving health equity.

Quality of care is another critical aspect of health policy. Policies that establish standards for healthcare delivery, monitor performance, and incentivize quality improvement can enhance the safety and effectiveness of care. Accreditation programs, quality measurement initiatives, and value-based payment models are examples of policy mechanisms that promote high-quality care. Continuous evaluation and adaptation of quality improvement policies are necessary to address emerging challenges and ensure that healthcare providers deliver optimal care.

Public health policies focus on preventing disease, promoting health, and protecting the well-being of communities. Vaccination programs, tobacco control policies, and efforts to address the social determinants of health are examples of public health initiatives that can significantly impact population health. Collaborative approaches that involve multiple sectors, such as education, housing, and transportation, are essential for addressing the complex factors that influence health. Advocacy efforts that raise awareness about public health issues and mobilize resources can drive policy changes and improve health outcomes.

Health system financing policies determine how healthcare services are funded and allocated. Sustainable financing mechanisms, such as progressive taxation, public insurance programs, and health savings accounts, can ensure that healthcare systems have the resources needed to provide comprehensive and equitable care. Policies that promote cost containment and efficient resource allocation can help address the rising costs of healthcare and ensure the long-term sustainability of health systems.

Advocacy is a powerful tool for influencing health policy and promoting positive change. Advocacy efforts can take many forms, including grass-roots organizing, public awareness campaigns, policy research, and direct engagement with policymakers. By amplifying the voices of those affected by health disparities and advocating for evidence-based policies, individuals and organizations can drive meaningful improvements in health outcomes. Building coalitions, leveraging media platforms, and fostering relationships with policymakers are key strategies for successful advocacy.

In summary, health policy and advocacy are essential for shaping the healthcare landscape and promoting health equity. By engaging in policy development, quality improvement, public health initiatives, and advocacy efforts, we can create a more just and equitable healthcare system that meets the needs of all individuals.

16

Chapter 16: The Future of Health and Commerce

As we look to the future, the intersection of health and commerce will continue to evolve, driven by advancements in technology, shifts in societal values, and emerging global challenges. The future of health and commerce holds both opportunities and uncertainties, requiring innovative approaches and collaborative efforts to navigate the complexities of a rapidly changing world.

Technology will play a central role in shaping the future of health and commerce. Innovations in artificial intelligence, biotechnology, and digital health will continue to transform healthcare delivery, disease prevention, and patient care. The integration of AI-driven diagnostics, personalized medicine, and telehealth services will enhance the accuracy, accessibility, and efficiency of healthcare. Wearable health devices and health apps will empower individuals to take a proactive role in managing their health, providing real-time data and personalized insights. However, addressing issues related to data privacy, cybersecurity, and equity will be critical to ensure the ethical and inclusive use of health technology.

The future of health will also be influenced by shifts in societal values and expectations. As people become more aware of the social determinants of health and the importance of health equity, there will be a growing

CHAPTER 16: THE FUTURE OF HEALTH AND COMMERCE

demand for policies and practices that promote social justice and inclusivity. Health systems will need to adopt a holistic approach that addresses the physical, mental, and social aspects of health. Emphasizing preventive care, community-based interventions, and patient-centered care will be essential for creating a more equitable and sustainable healthcare system.

Global challenges, such as climate change, pandemics, and economic instability, will continue to impact health and commerce. Climate change poses significant health risks, including the spread of vector-borne diseases, heat-related illnesses, and food and water insecurity. Preparing for and mitigating the health impacts of climate change will require coordinated efforts at the local, national, and global levels. The COVID-19 pandemic has highlighted the importance of robust public health infrastructure, international cooperation, and resilience in the face of health crises. Building resilient health systems that can respond effectively to emergencies and adapt to changing conditions will be crucial for ensuring public health and economic stability.

The future of commerce will be shaped by evolving consumer preferences and market dynamics. There will be a growing emphasis on sustainability, social responsibility, and ethical business practices. Companies that prioritize health and well-being, environmental sustainability, and corporate social responsibility will be better positioned to thrive in a competitive market. Consumers will increasingly seek products and services that align with their values, driving demand for healthier and more sustainable options. The integration of health and wellness into business models will become a key differentiator and a source of competitive advantage.

In summary, the future of health and commerce will be shaped by technological advancements, shifts in societal values, and global challenges. By embracing innovation, promoting health equity, and addressing emerging threats, we can create a future that supports the health and well-being of individuals and communities while fostering sustainable economic growth.

Chapter 17: The Path Forward: Integrating Health and Commerce for a Better Future

As we reach the conclusion of our exploration into the interplay between politics, society, psychology, and commerce, it becomes clear that a holistic and integrated approach is essential for fostering health and well-being. The path forward involves harnessing the synergies between these domains to create a healthier, more equitable, and sustainable future.

One of the key steps in this integration is the collaboration between stakeholders across sectors. Governments, businesses, healthcare providers, community organizations, and individuals all have a role to play in promoting health and well-being. Public-private partnerships can leverage the strengths and resources of both sectors to address complex health challenges. For example, collaborations between technology companies and healthcare providers can drive innovation in digital health, while partnerships between government agencies and community organizations can enhance public health initiatives. By working together, stakeholders can create comprehensive solutions that address the root causes of health issues and promote systemic change.

Policy coherence is another critical element in integrating health and commerce. Health policies should align with economic, social, and environmental policies to ensure a coordinated approach to health and well-being. For example, economic policies that promote job creation and financial stability can support mental health and reduce health disparities. Environmental policies that address air and water quality can prevent health problems and promote sustainability. Social policies that focus on education, housing, and social support can enhance the social determinants of health. By ensuring that policies across different sectors are aligned and mutually reinforcing, we can create a more supportive environment for health and well-being.

Investing in health is fundamental to driving economic growth and development. A healthy population is more productive, innovative, and resilient. Investments in healthcare infrastructure, medical research, and public health programs can yield significant economic returns by reducing healthcare costs, improving workforce productivity, and enhancing quality of life. Additionally, investments in education, social services, and environmental sustainability can create the conditions for long-term health and prosperity. Policymakers and business leaders must recognize the value of investing in health as a cornerstone of economic development.

Promoting health equity is essential for creating a just and inclusive society. Efforts to reduce health disparities must address the social determinants of health and ensure that all individuals have access to the resources and opportunities needed for good health. This includes providing affordable healthcare, improving educational and economic opportunities, and fostering supportive community environments. Health equity initiatives should be guided by principles of social justice, inclusivity, and cultural competence. By prioritizing health equity, we can ensure that the benefits of health and economic progress are shared by all members of society.

Innovation and adaptability are crucial for navigating the uncertainties and challenges of the future. Embracing new technologies, approaches, and models of care can drive progress and enhance health outcomes. However, it is essential to remain vigilant about the ethical, social, and equity implications of innovation. Ensuring that new advancements are accessible and beneficial to all individuals, regardless of their background or circumstances, is fundamental to creating a sustainable and equitable future.

In conclusion, the path forward involves integrating health and commerce through collaboration, policy coherence, investment, health equity, and innovation. By adopting a holistic and inclusive approach, we can create a future that supports the health and well-being of individuals and communities while fostering economic growth and sustainability. The journey toward a healthier and more prosperous world requires collective action, shared responsibility, and a commitment to the principles of justice, equity, and human dignity.

The Wellness Analogy: How Politics, Society, and Psychology Influence Health and Commerce

In "The Wellness Analogy," the intricate connections between politics, society, psychology, and commerce are explored to reveal their profound impact on health and well-being. This insightful book delves into how political decisions, societal norms, psychological factors, and economic policies shape health outcomes and influence the landscape of healthcare and commerce.

Each chapter unpacks a different dimension of this complex interplay, from the role of government policies in healthcare access to the influence of societal structures on mental health. The book examines the psychological underpinnings of health behaviors, the impact of globalization and technology on public health, and the crucial importance of health equity and social justice. Through comprehensive analyses and real-world examples, "The Wellness Analogy" offers a holistic understanding of how these interconnected factors contribute to the health of individuals and communities.

With a focus on collaboration, innovation, and policy coherence, the book underscores the need for integrated approaches to address contemporary health challenges. "The Wellness Analogy" provides valuable insights for policymakers, healthcare professionals, business leaders, and anyone interested in the intersection of health and societal dynamics. It serves as a call to action to create a healthier, more equitable, and sustainable future by leveraging the synergies between politics, society, psychology, and commerce.

www.ingramcontent.com/pod-product-compliance
Lightning Source LLC
LaVergne TN
LVHW020457080526
838202LV00057B/6004